ADVENTURES BEYOND BORDERS

ADVENTURES BEYOND BORDERS

A Digital Nomad's Journey to the New American Dream

MARCY SCHAAF

Children

CONTENTS

Title: Adventures Beyond Borders: A Digital Nomad's Journey to the New American Dream

Title: Adventures Beyond Borders:
A Digital Nomad's Journey to the New American Dream

Table of Content:

Introduction:

In a world marked by traditional expectations and conventional norms, there exists a remarkable narrative that challenges the status quo and invites readers to embark on a journey that transcends boundaries—both geographical and ideological. "Adventures Beyond Borders: A Digital Nomad's Journey to the New American Dream" is a compelling exploration of a life that defies limitations and embraces the ever-evolving landscape of the digital age.

Within the pages of this immersive narrative, we are introduced to the extraordinary lives of Lily, Max, and Mia—three young souls who, like so many of their generation, yearned for something more profound than the monotony of desk-bound careers and predetermined life trajectories. These young minds dared to dream, envisioning a life rich in adventures, abundant in learning experiences, and unshackled from the traditional confines of a classroom or office.

Their journey is not just a tale of wanderlust and exploration, but a testament to the power of the digital era—a time where freedom, knowledge, and unconventional paths beckon like never before. These young adventurers were not content with the ordinary; they sought the extraordinary. And in their quest, they discovered a new vision of the American dream, one that transcended the pursuit of material wealth and instead focused on the invaluable treasures of experience, connection, and fulfillment.

"Adventures Beyond Borders" invites readers to venture alongside Lily, Max, and Mia, embracing the world as their classroom and their compass. Each chapter of their journey unfolds as a lesson in life, offering insights into the art of breaking free from convention, of cherishing the beauty of diversity, and of savoring the simplicity that often eludes our hurried lives.

This narrative is not just a travelogue but a manifesto for a generation seeking a different kind of success—one that thrives on curiosity, passion, and the courage to break away from the ordinary. As these young digital nomads traverse continents, they explore the intricacies of finance, immerse themselves in the vibrant cultures of the world, and seek solace in the pursuit of happiness that transcends the pursuit of material possessions.

"Adventures Beyond Borders" is not just a story of self-discovery but a manual for those who yearn to embrace the new American dream—a dream that thrives in the world's enchanting landscapes, celebrates the richness of global diversity, and cherishes the allure of a life unburdened by the acquisition of material possessions.

Prepare to embark on a voyage that is bound to ignite the flames of curiosity, redefine your notion of the American dream, and inspire you to pursue the uncharted territories of life, knowledge, and experience. With "Adventures Beyond Borders," we invite you to join the ranks of those who choose to live life on their terms, unbounded by tradition, and enriched by the world's vast tapestry of experiences.

Chapter 1: The Quest for Freedom

In a quiet suburban neighborhood, there lived three children who yearned for something more than the confines of their daily lives. These were not your ordinary kids. Lily, Max, and Mia were dreamers. They possessed an insatiable curiosity and an unquenchable thirst for adventure. They had an idea that seemed almost magical in its audacity – the idea of becoming digital nomads.

The Quest Begins

Lily was the eldest at twelve. With her long, wavy hair and inquisitive brown eyes, she was the dreamer of the group. She'd often lay on her bedroom floor, staring at the posters of far-off destinations plastered on her walls. Her favorite book was a tattered atlas, and her daydreams revolved around exploring new cultures, breathing in the scents of exotic markets, and feeling the warm embrace of foreign lands.

Max was eleven, the middle child. He had a mop of unruly brown hair and a perpetual grin that could brighten anyone's day. Max loved technology and had a knack for understanding it. He could fix a computer faster than most adults and had a YouTube channel where he reviewed gadgets. But he wasn't content with just understanding the digital world; he wanted to see the real world.

Mia, at eight, was the youngest and the peacemaker of the group. Her sparkling blue eyes radiated innocence and joy. She could make friends with anyone, and her charm was her ticket to learning about different people and cultures. Mia often wondered why people didn't always get along. She believed that traveling the world and experiencing its diversity would help her find the answers.

Their Inspiration

The catalyst for this bold plan came when their school invited a world traveler to speak. He shared stories of his adventures across the globe, describing the vibrant colors of foreign markets, the deliciousness of unique cuisines, and the breathtaking beauty of natural wonders. He spoke of the people he met, the kindness he encountered, and the friends he made in faraway lands.

For Lily, Max, and Mia, these stories weren't just tales of far-off adventures but invitations to a world that lay beyond the horizon of their small town. The idea of becoming digital nomads, of traveling the world, learning from experiences rather than textbooks, took root in their minds.

The Idea Takes Shape

After the talk, the three friends gathered in Lily's cozy attic. It was here that they hatched their plan. Their heads were filled with the possibilities of a life less ordinary, a life that resembled the stories they had just heard.

Lily, ever the organizer, brought out her father's old world map. It hung on the wall, a silent witness to their dreams. "Why don't we mark all the places we want to visit?" she suggested, holding a colorful set of markers. Max and Mia nodded enthusiastically, and they began to pin destinations, imagining themselves standing on foreign soil.

They spoke about the subjects they could learn while traveling. Max suggested they study math through currency exchange. "We could learn economics, too," he said, "and understand what events affect currency rates." Mia was excited about studying geography by actually visiting the places. "No more looking at the globe; we can touch it!" she exclaimed.

The Talk with Their Parents

That evening, Lily, Max, and Mia approached their parents with their audacious plan. At first, there was skepticism and concern. Were they too young for such an adventure? What about school, friends, and the comfort of home? But the kids were persuasive, armed with their dreams, and the wisdom they'd gleaned from the world traveler's talk.

Their parents, seeing the passion and determination in their children's eyes, decided to give it a chance. They agreed to homeschool the children during their travels, provided they remained dedicated to learning. It was a momentous decision that would change the course of their lives.

The Beginning of an Adventure

The journey began with the trio setting out on their first adventure, exploring places within the United States. They drove across the country, visiting national parks, experiencing different climates, and learning about the rich diversity of their own country. Along the way, they learned how to navigate, cook, and budget. They also learned to appreciate the beauty of nature, the warmth of strangers, and the joy of wandering.

As the months passed, the three friends, now digital nomads in the making, started to explore international destinations. They discovered the art of navigating airports, learning phrases in foreign languages, and adapting to new cultures.

Chapter 1: The Quest for Freedom, marked the beginning of their exciting journey as digital nomads, where the walls of the traditional classroom transformed into the vast world, waiting to be explored. Their quest for freedom had just begun, and they were ready to embrace every lesson, experience, and adventure that lay ahead.

With each new destination, they grew wiser, more tolerant, and more in love with the idea of learning through experiences. The ordinary life they left behind seemed like a distant memory, replaced by a world of extraordinary possibilities. In the chapters that followed, they would explore the intricacies of currency exchange, delve into the wonders of geography, and discover the true meaning of happiness. But the most significant lesson of all was that the pursuit of freedom and knowledge could lead to the most extraordinary adventures of all.

Chapter 2: The World as Your Classroom

After their decision to become digital nomads, Lily, Max, and Mia set out on an extraordinary journey. Their mission: to turn the world into their classroom. They had chosen a life less conventional, but it was filled with the promise of unparalleled adventure and limitless learning opportunities. Chapter 2 would be all about the transformative power of exploring the world beyond the borders of the United States.

Lessons in Every Corner

Lily, Max, and Mia quickly discovered that the world was indeed their classroom, and that learning opportunities were everywhere. They were no longer limited to textbooks, blackboards, and scheduled classes. Instead, the world became a vast, open book waiting to be explored.

As they traveled, they couldn't help but notice that each new place held valuable lessons, teaching them something unique and inspiring. Even the simplest experiences, like savoring a bowl of pho on the bustling streets of Hanoi or strolling through the ancient streets of Rome, became part of their education.

In a small coastal village in Thailand, they learned about marine ecosystems and the importance of coral reefs. By volunteering with a local organization, they witnessed firsthand how pollution could harm the oceans and affect the livelihoods of the people who depended on them. The crystal-clear waters and colorful marine life served as a beautiful, yet fragile, lesson in environmental conservation.

In an ancient temple in Angkor Wat, Cambodia, they explored the intricacies of Hindu and Buddhist art and architecture, learning about the history and culture of Southeast Asia. The temple complex became a living textbook, with its stone carvings telling stories of a bygone era.

The Great Wall of China introduced them to the wonders of engineering and construction. They marveled at the sheer size and complexity of this ancient marvel, realizing that history and culture could be studied through the remarkable structures left behind by civilizations of the past.

Life on the Road

The trio adapted to a life on the road, embracing the challenges and learning opportunities it presented. They developed essential life skills as they moved from one place to another. Simple tasks, such as navigating public transportation in foreign cities, became valuable lessons in problem-solving and independence.

Their education extended beyond traditional subjects. They learned about responsibility by planning their travels and managing their finances. Budgeting became a critical skill as they discovered that making wise choices allowed them to continue their adventures for longer.

Through their travels, they learned practical skills as well. Max became an expert at setting up campfires, while Mia's cooking skills expanded as she tried her hand at preparing diverse cuisines from around the world. They didn't just learn to cook; they learned about the ingredients, flavors, and the cultural significance of each dish.

Friendships and Connections

One of the most beautiful aspects of their journey was the connections they made along the way. From the friendly fruit vendor in a Vietnamese market to the fellow travelers they met in hostels, Lily, Max, and Mia learned that human connections were as important as any lesson from a textbook. They interacted with people from different walks of life, sparking conversations about culture, traditions, and dreams.

These encounters taught them about the importance of tolerance and understanding. They began to see that despite language barriers and cultural differences, there was an underlying thread of shared humanity that connected them to people from all corners of the world.

In Rome, they made friends with a local family who invited them to dinner in their home. Through the laughter, shared stories, and the taste of homemade pasta, they experienced the warmth of Italian hospitality. The bond they formed transcended borders, leaving an indelible mark on their hearts.

Learning Through Observation

The children found that simply observing the world around them was a valuable form of learning. The vibrant markets in Marrakech, Morocco, taught them about economics, trade, and the art of haggling. They would spend hours watching the flurry of activity, fascinated by the intricate dance of buying and selling.

In Peru, they learned about agriculture by visiting local farms and observing the techniques used to grow crops in high-altitude regions. They realized that education extended far beyond textbooks and that knowledge could be gathered by watching and engaging with the world.

Geography and History Unveiled

The map on Lily's bedroom wall started to come to life as they visited the places they had marked. They stood in front of the Eiffel Tower in Paris, strolled through the narrow lanes of Kyoto, Japan, and witnessed the grandeur of the Pyramids in Egypt. Geography transformed from an abstract concept into a tangible reality. They didn't just read about the world; they experienced it.

History, too, was no longer confined to the pages of textbooks. As they explored ancient ruins, walked along the remnants of the Berlin Wall, and visited war museums, they encountered the stories of humanity's past. Each historical site became a chapter in their personal history book, a tangible connection to the events that had shaped the world.

Cultures and Languages

As they immersed themselves in new cultures, they learned to appreciate the diversity of the world. In Tokyo, they witnessed the grace of a traditional tea ceremony and learned about the intricacies of Japanese culture. In India, they celebrated Diwali, the Festival of Lights, and learned about Hindu traditions.

Learning languages became an adventure in itself. They picked up phrases in each country they visited, and slowly but surely, they began to communicate with locals. Language became a bridge that allowed them to connect on a deeper level with the people they met.

Living a Multifaceted Education

The world as their classroom taught Lily, Max, and Mia that life was a multifaceted education. They realized that traditional classrooms were only one way of learning and that experiences were equally, if not more, valuable. They had discovered that the world was their greatest teacher, and each day held a new lesson.

As they moved forward in their journey, they understood that the world had so much more to offer. Their education was ongoing, and the adventure was far from over. They had embraced a life of wonder, exploration, and learning, and they couldn't wait to see what new chapters awaited them in the world as their ever-expansive classroom. Chapter 2 had only just begun, and the pages of their story were ready to be filled with the knowledge, experiences, and connections that the world had in store for them.

Chapter 3: Math on the Move

As Lily, Max, and Mia continued their journey, they realized that math wasn't confined to the pages of a textbook or the walls of a classroom. It was all around them, and the world became their living math lesson. In this chapter, they embarked on a fascinating adventure of discovering math on the move and, most intriguingly, the world of currency exchange. They began to understand that not only did math serve as a practical tool for daily life while traveling, but it also held the key to unlocking the mysteries of economics, currency values, and the fascinating ways money worked across the globe.

Currency Exchange: Unveiling the World of Finance

Their first lesson in the world of currency exchange began when they crossed the border into Canada. The familiar greenbacks in their wallets transformed into colorful Canadian dollars. At that moment, they realized that money, just like math, took on a different form and value in different parts of the world.

Max, with his innate tech-savviness, had a collection of currency conversion apps at his fingertips. He explained to Lily and Mia how these tools helped them understand the value of their money in any given country. For the first time, math became not just about numbers but a means to navigate the global financial landscape.

The concept of currency exchange fascinated the trio. They discovered that currencies were subject to economic factors, including inflation rates, interest rates, and government policies. The value of a currency could change from one day to the next, and understanding these fluctuations became essential for budgeting and making financial decisions while on the move.

The USD's Peculiar Powers

One of the intriguing aspects of their journey was that the U.S. dollar (USD) held a unique position in the world of currency exchange. They learned that the USD was considered a strong and stable currency, which meant that it often held more value than the local currencies of the countries they visited.

This knowledge served them well, as they found that their USD could go a long way in some countries. Countries like Grenada, Italy, Mexico, and Egypt were among the places where the USD's value was notably higher than the local currencies. The trio quickly realized the practical advantages of this financial insight.

In Grenada, a beautiful Caribbean destination, the USD was widely accepted, and its exchange rate was quite favorable. They found that their dollars stretched further, enabling them to enjoy more meals, activities, and experiences. As they hiked through lush rainforests and lounged on the picturesque beaches, they could appreciate the financial wisdom of understanding the currency market.

In Italy, the USD's advantage became evident as they savored delicious Italian cuisine, explored the ruins of Rome, and admired the art in Florence. The strong USD meant that they could afford to experience Italy's rich culture and history without breaking the bank.

Mexico, with its vibrant culture and stunning beaches, was another country where their dollars went a long way. The trio marveled at the colorful markets, indulged in mouthwatering street food, and dived into the crystal-clear waters of the Yucatan Peninsula. Their knowledge of currency exchange allowed them to make the most of their Mexican adventure.

In Egypt, the ancient wonders of the world beckoned, and their USD offered a significant advantage. They explored the pyramids, cruised the Nile, and marveled at the intricate hieroglyphics on ancient temples, all while appreciating the economic benefits of a strong currency.

The Value of Financial Knowledge

Understanding currency exchange rates wasn't just about getting more value for their money; it also provided a valuable lesson in economics. The kids began to appreciate the complexities of global financial systems and how economic factors could impact the value of a currency. They learned that international trade, government policies, and even political stability could influence exchange rates.

As they continued their journey, they encountered situations where knowing the currency exchange rates made a significant difference. They navigated through bustling markets, haggled with vendors, and made informed choices about where to exchange their USD for the best rates. Each transaction became a practical math lesson, helping them sharpen their money management skills.

Budgeting and Financial Responsibility

The financial knowledge they gained had a more profound impact on their journey than they initially realized. It wasn't just about enjoying more ice cream or souvenirs; it was about responsible budgeting and managing their resources effectively.

They developed the habit of keeping meticulous records of their expenses, tracking their spending in various currencies. This allowed them to plan for future destinations, allocate funds for accommodations, activities, and food, and ensure they stayed within their budget.

Max, the tech guru, created a digital spreadsheet that automatically updated the exchange rates, helping them make informed financial decisions. They also researched and used local banking services to minimize currency exchange fees.

The Power of Practical Math

Beyond currency exchange, practical math was woven into their daily lives. They used math to calculate distances, time zones, and the cost of transportation. They solved real-world problems such as determining the amount of fuel needed for a road trip, managing their time effectively to catch trains and flights, and calculating tips for service personnel.

Mia's love for cooking provided further opportunities for math. She converted recipes from one unit of measurement to another, learning about the metric system in the process. Her culinary adventures allowed her to understand the importance of precision in measurements.

The Math of It All

Chapter 3 marked a significant point in their journey as they explored the intricate world of currency exchange and practical math. They realized that math wasn't just a subject in school; it was an essential tool for navigating the complexities of a global adventure.

The knowledge of currency exchange, coupled with an understanding of the USD's strength in certain countries, empowered them to make wise financial decisions. They recognized the value of responsible budgeting and financial planning, and how practical math could lead to a more enriching travel experience.

As they continued their travels, they were ready to embrace the world with newfound financial wisdom. Chapter 3 was not only about the math of currency exchange but also the transformation of their perspective on the global economy and how it could shape their journey. Armed with practical math and a strong USD, they were ready to embark on even more adventures and uncover the endless lessons the world had in store for them.

Chapter 4: Geography Unfolded

As Lily, Max, and Mia continued their remarkable journey as digital nomads, their world opened up in ways they could have never imagined. In Chapter 4, the young adventurers delved into the fascinating realm of geography, experiencing firsthand the beauty and diversity of the world's landscapes, cultures, and histories. Geography was no longer a dry subject studied in a classroom; it was a vibrant tapestry that they touched, felt, and lived.

Traveling to the Locations

Their atlas came to life as they embarked on a journey to visit the locations they had marked. They had already discovered that geography was more than just learning the names of countries and their capitals; it was about exploring the unique characteristics of each place, understanding the people who called those locations home, and appreciating the natural wonders and historical sites that made the world so captivating.

Lily, Max, and Mia were fortunate to have the opportunity to explore a wide range of destinations, each offering a new lesson in geography.

Europe's Rich Tapestry

Europe was their first overseas adventure, where the concept of geography unfolded in magnificent ways. They strolled through the cobblestone streets of Paris, gazing upon the Eiffel Tower and the Louvre, marveling at the history and artistry of this beautiful city. They also visited the Swiss Alps, where towering peaks and sparkling lakes presented a geography lesson like no other. The kids understood that geography wasn't just about maps; it was about the impact of natural landscapes on the lives of the people who lived there.

Their journey took them to Venice, where they explored a city built on water and learned about the challenges of living in a unique geographic location. Then, they traveled to the ancient city of Athens, walking in the footsteps of philosophers, understanding the importance of geography in the birth of democracy.

In the fjords of Norway, the trio marveled at the incredible geography of steep cliffs and crystal-clear waters. It was a lesson in natural wonders, demonstrating the forces of nature that had shaped these landscapes over millions of years.

The Unique Geography of Asia

The vast continent of Asia introduced them to geography on a grand scale. They explored the bustling streets of Tokyo, with its mix of modern architecture and traditional shrines, learning how urban geography played a vital role in city planning and culture. In Kyoto, they discovered the historical heart of Japan, where geography had a profound influence on the city's layout and traditions.

Traveling through the diverse landscapes of China, from the bustling streets of Beijing to the serene rice terraces of Guilin, they realized how geography had shaped China's culture, agriculture, and history. The Great Wall of China, a colossal feat of human geography, was a testament to the power of geography as both a defensive structure and a symbol of a united empire.

Exploring the Gobi Desert in Mongolia taught them about the geography of arid landscapes, nomadic cultures, and the adaptability of those who called such places home.

Ancient Wonders and Cultural Marvels

Their journey brought them to Egypt, where they marveled at the Pyramids of Giza. The trio learned how geography played a critical role in the location of these ancient marvels, not just for religious purposes but also as a testament to the engineering and architectural skills of the time.

In India, the geographical diversity was astonishing. They explored the Thar Desert in Rajasthan, witnessed the lush beauty of Kerala's backwaters, and experienced the vibrancy of Mumbai. India's geography was a living kaleidoscope, offering lessons in climate, biodiversity, and human adaptation.

South America's Natural Splendors

South America was a geography lover's paradise. They hiked the Inca Trail to Machu Picchu, appreciating the geography of high-altitude terrains and the ancient city's strategic location. They ventured into the Amazon Rainforest, understanding the critical role of geography in sustaining one of the most biodiverse regions on Earth.

Galápagos Islands provided them with a lesson in unique biogeography, with each island showcasing a distinct ecosystem and species that had evolved in isolation. The Galápagos Islands were a living testament to the theory of evolution and the geographical isolation that had contributed to it.

North America's Grandeur

Back in North America, the kids explored the grandeur of Yellowstone National Park, with its geothermal wonders, including geysers, hot springs, and mudpots. They learned about the geological forces that shaped the park's extraordinary features and the importance of protecting such natural wonders.

In Canada, they encountered the stunning landscapes of Banff and Jasper National Parks. The towering Rocky Mountains, crystal-clear lakes, and abundant wildlife were all part of a geography lesson in the forces that had created these dramatic landscapes.

Learning Beyond Maps

Geography wasn't just about physical landscapes; it also encompassed human geography. As the kids traveled through various countries and interacted with locals, they began to understand how geography influenced human settlements, lifestyles, and cultural practices.

In Japan, they observed how a densely populated country had found unique ways to maximize space and efficiency in urban areas. In rural Mongolia, they learned about nomadic herding cultures and the geographic factors that drove this way of life.

The geography of climate and weather patterns became evident as they experienced diverse weather conditions in different parts of the world. They learned about monsoons in India, the dry deserts of Egypt, and the seasonal changes in Europe and North America.

Natural Forces and Sustainability

Geography was not only about the past and present but also about the future. The kids discovered the importance of understanding the Earth's geography to address critical issues such as climate change, sustainability, and conservation. They encountered projects focused on preserving ecosystems, reducing pollution, and maintaining the delicate balance of natural geography.

The geography of natural disasters also became a sobering lesson. They experienced earthquakes in Japan, monsoon flooding in India, and wildfires in the United States. These encounters made them acutely aware of the need for preparedness, disaster relief, and understanding the geographical factors that influenced such events.

A Journey of Endless Discovery

Chapter 4: Geography Unfolded marked a chapter of limitless discovery. As Lily, Max, and Mia roamed the world, they realized that geography wasn't just a subject to be studied but a living, breathing entity that shaped the planet's landscapes, cultures, and histories.

Their atlas transformed from a collection of pages into a vibrant tapestry that told the stories of diverse regions, people, and ecosystems. Geography became a passport to the world, allowing them to explore the Earth's marvels and appreciate the beauty of its intricate design.

With each step they took, they unveiled new layers of knowledge that deepened their appreciation for the planet. Geography was no longer a set of facts to memorize; it was the essence of their journey, guiding them through the enchanting diversity of the world and encouraging them to continue exploring, one destination at a time.

Chapter 5: Tolerance and Understanding

In the realm of their global journey, Lily, Max, and Mia, the intrepid trio of young digital nomads, found themselves not only exploring exotic landscapes and savoring foreign cuisines but also navigating the intricate terrain of human diversity. Chapter 5 of their adventure, "Tolerance and Understanding," sheds light on their remarkable transformation as they crossed paths with people of different cultures, backgrounds, and traditions.

From the moment they departed the familiar shores of the United States, Lily, Max, and Mia embarked on a transformative journey of cultural exploration. The world, it seemed, was more than just a playground of geographical wonders; it was also a vast tapestry of humanity, woven from the threads of countless unique cultures. This diversity would become the crucible where their tolerance and understanding would be forged.

One of the first lessons the young nomads learned was that, in a world brimming with diversity, assumptions and stereotypes can be deceptive. Lily, with her vibrant auburn hair and freckles, and Max, with his infectious curiosity, initially carried with them a set of preconceived notions about how people from various parts of the world would act and interact. Mia, with her deep appreciation for history and culture, often served as their guide on this eye-opening journey.

Their first true encounter with cultural diversity took place in the bustling streets of Tokyo, Japan. Here, amid neon signs and the hum of a metropolis, the trio quickly realized that their American customs and expectations didn't always translate smoothly. The Japanese bow, for instance, was more than a polite gesture; it was a reflection of respect, and Mia, always eager to dive deep into cultural nuances, explained the significance of these customs.

As they ventured further into their journey, they found themselves in India, where they encountered a vibrant tapestry of languages, religions, and traditions. India was a land of contrasts, where ancient temples and bustling markets coexisted. Here, the trio learned the importance of respecting religious diversity, attending a Diwali celebration, and visiting the majestic temples and mosques that peppered the landscape. Mia's knowledge proved invaluable as she explained the significance of the different festivals and rituals they witnessed.

But it wasn't all rosy. They faced cultural misunderstandings that tested their newfound tolerance and understanding. In Morocco, their hosts welcomed them with mint tea, a symbol of hospitality. However, Lily, Max, and Mia were initially taken aback by the intense sweetness. They had to remind themselves of the importance of embracing differences and respecting local customs, even when they were outside their comfort zone. Over time, they developed a deeper appreciation for the rich flavors of Moroccan cuisine.

The true test of their growing tolerance and understanding came in their encounter with a Bedouin family in the deserts of Jordan. The Bedouins were known for their hospitality, and the young nomads found themselves invited to share a meal and stay in a traditional desert tent. The simple, nomadic lifestyle of their hosts was a stark contrast to their upbringing in the United States.

Lily, Max, and Mia observed as the Bedouin family, led by an elderly patriarch, went about their daily routines, tending to their camels, preparing traditional meals, and sharing stories around a campfire under the starlit desert sky. Mia, who was the most intrigued by history, learned about the Bedouin culture and their enduring connection to the land.

This experience challenged their understanding of what constituted a fulfilling life. They realized that happiness was not solely dependent on material possessions or a fixed, sedentary lifestyle. The Bedouins, with their rich culture and strong sense of community, demonstrated that simplicity and connection to one's roots could bring profound contentment.

In the following chapters of their journey, the trio continued to engage with diverse communities, from the indigenous tribes of the Amazon Rainforest to the colorful markets of Marrakech. They came to understand that the world was a mosaic of cultures, and the people they met along the way enriched their lives in countless ways.

Their adventures also highlighted the universal human qualities that transcended borders and languages. Laughter, love, and the pursuit of happiness were themes they encountered in every corner of the globe. The bonds they formed with people from different cultures were a testament to the power of human connection.

Chapter 5, "Tolerance and Understanding," was not just a lesson in cultural awareness; it was a revelation of the fundamental truth that diversity is the essence of humanity. The young nomads learned that by embracing differences and celebrating what makes each culture unique, they could expand their own horizons and gain a deeper understanding of the world.

As Lily, Max, and Mia continued their journey, they carried the lessons of tolerance and understanding with them, making it a mission to bridge cultural gaps and foster connections wherever they went. Their story serves as a reminder that in a world marked by differences, it is the bonds we create and the bridges we build that define our shared humanity.

Chapter 6: The Culinary Chronicles

As Lily, Max, and Mia continued their global adventure, the chapter titled "The Culinary Chronicles" unfolded a delightful journey through the world of flavors, ingredients, and culinary traditions. It was a chapter that not only tantalized their taste buds but also shed light on the remarkable differences in culinary practices and their consequences on health and longevity.

One of the most fascinating aspects of their journey was the way each country's cuisine revealed a unique facet of its culture. In exploring food, they were also exploring the soul of the people they met, and they began to realize that there was much more to a dish than just its taste. It was a window into the history, traditions, and values of each nation.

Throughout their travels, Lily, Max, and Mia savored diverse dishes, from the exquisite sushi in Japan to the fragrant curries of India. Each meal brought with it a lesson not just in flavor but in culture and sustainability.

While their journey through food was a delicious exploration, it also unveiled a sobering reality - the impact of food production on health and longevity. As they dined in various countries, the young nomads couldn't help but notice the stark contrast between the ingredients used in different regions, especially in comparison to their own experiences back in the United States.

It was in Italy that the trio first grasped the importance of fresh, locally sourced ingredients. They enjoyed the simple yet incredibly flavorful dishes that the Italian cuisine had to offer. They learned that Italian cuisine was founded on the principle of using the freshest, most wholesome ingredients available. The practice of farm-to-table eating was deeply ingrained in the culture, and it reflected in the longevity of the Italian people.

Mia, who was deeply interested in the cultural aspects of food, explained how the Mediterranean diet, rich in olive oil, fresh vegetables, and lean proteins, had contributed to Italy's reputation for long and healthy lives. The importance of a balanced diet in promoting health and longevity became evident, and the trio found themselves wondering about the dietary choices they'd grown up with in the United States.

Their culinary journey led them to countries like Greece, where they marveled at the exquisite salads and seafood, and Thailand, where they discovered the vibrant world of street food. In these countries, the abundance of fresh, locally grown produce was evident, and the absence of highly processed foods was striking.

The stark contrast they encountered in the United States was brought to the forefront during their visit to a farmers' market in France. Here, they marveled at the rainbow of fresh produce, locally sourced meats, and artisanal cheeses. The idea of "farm-to-table" dining was not just a trend; it was a way of life.

Intrigued, they delved into the topic of food production and the impact of genetically modified organisms (GMOs) and pesticides on food quality and health. They learned that in some countries they visited, such as France, there were strict regulations and even bans on GMOs and certain pesticides. This was in stark contrast to the situation in the United States, where GMOs and pesticides were widely used in agriculture.

Mia, who had been researching the subject, explained how GMOs had been a topic of debate worldwide due to concerns about their potential long-term health effects. In some of the countries they visited, the precautionary principle was followed, and GMOs were either heavily regulated or banned altogether to ensure the safety of food.

Furthermore, in countries like France, they were amazed to find that there were restrictions on the use of certain pesticides, some of which had been linked to health issues like cancer and other chronic diseases. The trio began to understand the potential impact of these differences in regulations on the health and longevity of the people in these countries.

Their culinary explorations took them to regions of the world where the inhabitants seemed to enjoy a higher quality of life and longer lifespans. In Japan, they savored the freshest sushi and learned about the health benefits of the Japanese diet. Fish, vegetables, and fermented foods were staples, and the absence of heavily processed foods contributed to Japan's reputation for longevity.

Their journey also brought them to the picturesque Greek islands, where they tasted the vibrant flavors of olives, fruits, and the Mediterranean diet. They discovered the significance of a diet rich in antioxidants and healthy fats, and how it contributed to the well-being of the people in these regions.

Their experiences in Italy, where they indulged in traditional pasta dishes and fresh salads, revealed that a diet built around whole, unprocessed foods could not only satisfy the palate but also promote health and longevity. Italy's reputation as one of the healthiest countries in the world, with a diet centered on local, seasonal produce, began to make sense.

As they continued their journey, the trio encountered regions where diets were deeply rooted in tradition and community. In Morocco, they sampled flavorful tagines and learned about the health benefits of spices like saffron and cumin. These spices not only added depth to the cuisine but also offered medicinal properties that had been embraced for centuries.

The chapter on "The Culinary Chronicles" was more than just a culinary tour; it was an exploration of the relationship between food, culture, and health. The experiences of Lily, Max, and Mia highlighted how the choices people made in their diets and food production practices could have a profound impact on their overall well-being and longevity.

Their encounters with countries that imposed strict regulations on GMOs and pesticides raised thought-provoking questions about the role of government policies in shaping the health of a nation. While they didn't claim to have all the answers, their journey emphasized the significance of food choices in promoting not only the pleasures of the palate but also a healthier and longer life.

In their ongoing quest to discover the new American dream, the young nomads had encountered a powerful reminder that a significant part of the dream was intertwined with the food they ate and the choices they made in their culinary adventures. They would carry this knowledge with them as they continued to explore the world and learn from the diverse cultures and cuisines they encountered along the way.

Chapter 7: The Pursuit of Happiness

As Lily, Max, and Mia journeyed through the diverse cultures and cuisines of the world, they were increasingly drawn to an exploration that transcended geographical boundaries. This exploration was not of physical places, but of a deeply profound and universal theme - the pursuit of happiness. Chapter 7, "The Pursuit of Happiness," became a transformative leg of their journey, where they discovered that true contentment resided not in the accumulation of material things but in the intangible experiences that enriched their lives.

The young nomads had witnessed the allure of material possessions in their home country, the United States. A consumer-driven society, it often seemed as though happiness was equated with the latest gadgets, designer labels, and lavish lifestyles. It was an image of the American dream that was frequently projected in the media and advertising. Yet, it was a dream that appeared increasingly shallow and elusive, prompting the trio to venture beyond the borders in search of a deeper and more authentic happiness.

One of the first lessons they learned about happiness occurred in the rural villages of Thailand, where they encountered people who lived with far less material wealth than they had grown accustomed to. Here, amidst the tranquil rice paddies and humble bamboo huts, they found a sense of contentment and joy that defied conventional Western notions of success.

Lily, Max, and Mia observed the local communities engaging in simple yet meaningful activities - sharing meals, participating in festivals, and cherishing moments with their families. They realized that these villagers had a profound connection to each other and their environment, which contributed to a deep sense of fulfillment and happiness.

One evening, the trio joined a local family in preparing a traditional Thai meal. They chopped vegetables, ground herbs and spices, and cooked over an open flame. As they sat on the floor, sharing stories and savoring the meal they had prepared together, they experienced a sense of happiness that was far removed from the pursuit of material possessions.

Their journey through Asia took them to Bhutan, a country known for prioritizing Gross National Happiness (GNH) over Gross Domestic Product (GDP). Bhutan's unique approach to measuring its citizens' well-being placed a strong emphasis on spiritual, physical, and emotional well-being, rather than economic wealth.

In Bhutan, the young nomads explored the concept of happiness through interactions with monks and the practice of mindfulness and meditation. They learned that, for the Bhutanese, happiness was intimately tied to their sense of community, environmental conservation, and the pursuit of inner peace.

Mia, who had always been fascinated by the philosophy of happiness, noted that the Bhutanese people viewed the pursuit of material wealth as a path to suffering. Their unique perspective on happiness emphasized the importance of balance and inner fulfillment over material accumulation.

Their travels also brought them to the Blue Zones of Okinawa, Japan, and Ikaria, Greece, where they encountered communities renowned for their extraordinary longevity and high levels of happiness. Here, the focus was on simplicity, healthy diets, and strong social connections.

In Okinawa, the young nomads met elderly individuals who radiated vitality and happiness. These centenarians credited their longevity and contentment to a lifestyle that embraced active engagement with the community, a predominantly plant-based diet, and the practice of Ikigai, a sense of purpose in life.

In Ikaria, Greece, the trio found another community where people aged gracefully and joyfully. They discovered that the residents of this remote island placed a premium on relaxed living, a diet rich in fresh produce and olive oil, and the importance of strong social bonds. It was here that they encountered the phrase "hamenos" or "full of life," which epitomized the vibrant spirit of the Ikarian people.

Their experiences in these unique pockets of the world taught them that true happiness wasn't a product of wealth or the accumulation of material possessions. It was about cultivating strong connections with others, embracing simplicity, finding purpose in life, and fostering a sense of belonging.

It was in this chapter that Lily, Max, and Mia reflected on the role of material possessions and how they could often lead to emptiness and disillusionment. They realized that the pursuit of materialism could be a relentless cycle that left people perpetually seeking the next acquisition, often at the cost of their time, relationships, and overall well-being.

In contrast to this materialistic approach, they encountered communities where happiness was derived from the abundance of meaningful experiences, genuine connections with others, and the enrichment of the soul. These were places where people treasured their time, lived in harmony with nature, and focused on what truly mattered.

Their understanding of happiness deepened as they observed the diminishing returns of materialism in many Western societies, where conspicuous consumption often masked deeper issues of anxiety and unhappiness. The chapter underscored the importance of shifting the focus from external gains to internal well-being.

Throughout their travels, Lily, Max, and Mia began to embrace the notion that true happiness resided in the simple joys of life, such as sharing meals with loved ones, finding purpose in their journey, and forming meaningful connections with people from different cultures. Their experiences encouraged them to reflect on the values they had grown up with in the United States and question the relentless pursuit of material possessions.

As they continued their quest for the new American dream, they understood that this dream was not rooted in the acquisition of wealth or the possession of material things. It was about the pursuit of happiness in its purest form, a happiness that couldn't be bought, but only discovered within the heart and soul.

Chapter 7, "The Pursuit of Happiness," became a profound reminder that true contentment could be found in the richness of experiences, in the embrace of simplicity, and in the cultivation of authentic connections. The pursuit of happiness was no longer a distant dream; it was a journey they were living every day, a journey that led them to the heart of what it meant to be truly content and fulfilled.

Chapter 8: Nomadic Life on a Budget

As Lily, Max, and Mia continued their journey as digital nomads, they found themselves facing a fascinating challenge - navigating the world of nomadic life on a budget. Chapter 8, "Nomadic Life on a Budget," became a treasure trove of knowledge as they explored ways to travel affordably, manage their expenses, and even find free accommodations using platforms like Worldpackers and Workaway.

Their quest for a budget-friendly nomadic lifestyle began with a realization that long-term travel didn't have to be synonymous with extravagant expenses. In fact, it could be quite the opposite if approached strategically.

One of the most significant revelations was the trio's newfound understanding of the value of experiences over possessions. While the world was inundated with advertisements promoting the latest gadgets and designer labels, their travels showed them that the most rewarding and enriching aspects of life were often intangible.

They had encountered people across the globe who led content, fulfilling lives with minimal material possessions. This knowledge transformed their perspective, and they began to appreciate the importance of mindful spending and the significance of prioritizing experiences over material items.

One of the first lessons they learned about budget travel was the importance of setting a clear financial plan. This plan allowed them to outline their expenses, establish a budget, and track their spending. It was a simple yet powerful tool that ensured they could balance their wanderlust with financial responsibility.

The trio discovered that one of the most significant expenses during travel was accommodation. Staying in hotels and resorts could quickly deplete their budget, prompting them to seek alternative solutions. That's when they stumbled upon platforms like Worldpackers and Workaway.

Worldpackers and Workaway were transformative discoveries in their quest for budget-friendly travel. These platforms connected travelers with hosts offering accommodation in exchange for a few hours of work per day. The types of work varied greatly, from volunteering in organic farms to helping with hostel management, teaching English, or even assisting with social projects.

One of their most memorable experiences through Worldpackers was on a farm in Portugal. Here, they worked alongside locals, cultivating organic crops, and tending to animals. In return for their efforts, they received free accommodation and meals, immersing themselves in the local culture and gaining a deeper appreciation for sustainable living.

Their time with Workaway took them to a remote village in Nepal, where they volunteered at a local school. Their tasks included teaching English, assisting with daily chores, and even organizing extracurricular activities. In exchange for their help, they were welcomed into the homes of the local community and provided with free accommodation and meals.

The experiences with Worldpackers and Workaway not only significantly reduced their expenses but also enriched their journey by fostering connections with local communities. They learned that these platforms were not just about budget travel but were also about cultural immersion and authentic experiences.

As the trio explored these budget-friendly options, they also adopted a frugal mindset in their day-to-day expenses. They realized that by making conscious choices, they could save a significant amount of money without compromising the quality of their experiences.

One of the strategies they employed was cooking their meals. While indulging in local cuisines was an essential part of their journey, they also appreciated the value of preparing their food. Not only did it save money, but it also allowed them to explore local markets, experiment with new recipes, and connect with locals over shared culinary experiences.

Lily, with her love for research, often found local markets and street food vendors that offered delicious and affordable meals. In bustling markets, they savored exotic flavors and met local vendors who shared their culinary secrets. These experiences became not just about saving money but also about exploring the heart of a destination through its food.

Transportation costs were another significant consideration in their budget. They quickly learned to utilize various travel resources to secure affordable transport options. They embraced public transportation, shared rides, and even the occasional bicycle rental to explore their surroundings. These choices not only saved money but also allowed them to experience the world at a slower and more intimate pace.

The trio's quest for a budget-friendly nomadic life also led them to consider alternative forms of accommodation. They occasionally opted for hostels or guesthouses, which often offered reasonable rates and opportunities to connect with fellow travelers. They discovered that shared dorms and communal spaces were not just about saving money but also about forging new friendships and sharing travel stories.

Another cost-saving strategy they employed was traveling during the shoulder seasons or off-peak times. They found that airfare, accommodations, and tourist activities were often more affordable during these periods, and the destinations were less crowded, allowing for a more authentic and peaceful experience.

Throughout their journey, they consistently focused on experiences that didn't require spending significant amounts of money. They indulged in activities like hiking, exploring local neighborhoods, attending free cultural events, and immersing themselves in nature. They found that many of the most memorable experiences they had were completely free of charge.

The realization that they didn't need expensive material possessions to be happy became a guiding principle in their quest for a budget-friendly nomadic lifestyle. They recognized that the pursuit of endless possessions often led to a cycle of stress, debt, and the loss of freedom. Their journey became a testament to the joy of living a simpler and more fulfilling life, where each day was an adventure and each moment was an opportunity for learning and growth.

In their pursuit of happiness on a budget, Lily, Max, and Mia had come to understand that the richness of life didn't reside in the accumulation of material things. It was about experiences, connections, and the beauty of simplicity. Their encounters with platforms like Worldpackers and Workaway had opened doors to budget-friendly travel while offering opportunities to immerse themselves in local cultures and communities.

The chapter on "Nomadic Life on a Budget" was a testament to their realization that the pursuit of happiness didn't require a hefty bank account but rather a mindful approach to spending, a willingness to embrace simplicity, and a deep appreciation for the value of experiences over possessions.

As they continued their journey, they would carry these lessons with them, sharing the knowledge that a fulfilling and budget-friendly nomadic life was not just a possibility but a reality that could be achieved by anyone with the right mindset and a passion for the world.

Chapter 9: Follow Your Passions

In the unfolding narrative of Lily, Max, and Mia's remarkable journey as digital nomads, there came a pivotal chapter that revolved around a profound concept - "Follow Your Passions." This chapter became a testament to the importance of pursuing one's dreams, embracing the spirit of lifelong learning, and stepping out of one's comfort zone in the relentless quest for fulfillment and self-discovery.

The trio's journey had already been marked by encounters with diverse cultures, culinary delights, and the pursuit of happiness. However, they also embarked on a personal journey, a voyage into the depths of their own passions and dreams. As they traveled the world, they discovered that the pursuit of one's passions was not only achievable but an essential part of the human experience.

Lily, with her adventurous spirit and curiosity, had always been passionate about the environment and conservation. As they traveled through South America, she found herself immersed in opportunities to explore her love for nature and sustainability. This chapter saw her volunteering in the Amazon Rainforest, where she participated in reforestation efforts and wildlife conservation projects.

Her experiences deepened her connection to the natural world, instilling in her a profound appreciation for the delicate balance of ecosystems and the importance of preserving our planet. The lush and diverse landscapes of the Amazon, combined with the knowledge she gained, left an indelible mark on her heart and transformed her passion into a mission.

Max, who had always been a technology enthusiast, had long dreamed of creating innovative solutions that would have a positive impact on society. During their journey through Southeast Asia, he had the opportunity to connect with local tech communities and explore his passion for programming and entrepreneurship.

He collaborated with local startups and tech initiatives, contributing his skills and gaining invaluable experiences in return. These opportunities not only allowed him to follow his passion but also to learn from experts and immerse himself in a world of innovation and problem-solving.

Mia, who had a deep love for history, culture, and storytelling, used their travels as a canvas to explore her passion. She delved into local traditions, documented their journey, and shared their experiences through writing. She found herself interviewing local artisans, chronicling the stories of remote communities, and even participating in cultural events.

Her passion for storytelling allowed her to not only share the stories of the people they encountered but also to enrich their own journey with a deeper understanding of the places they visited. It was a reminder that following one's passion was not just a personal endeavor but also a way to connect with others and create a ripple effect of positive change.

One of the central themes of "Follow Your Passions" was the concept of lifelong learning. The trio realized that in following their passions, they had become lifelong learners, continually seeking knowledge and expanding their horizons. They embraced every opportunity to learn from the people they met, the places they explored, and the experiences they encountered.

The concept of lifelong learning had been woven into the very fabric of their journey. They attended local workshops, language classes, and cultural events, all of which allowed them to immerse themselves in the world of learning. The knowledge they acquired wasn't limited to textbooks or classrooms; it was experiential, dynamic, and rooted in real-life encounters.

Their journey reminded them that learning was not confined to a specific age, stage, or place. It was a lifelong endeavor that could be pursued with passion and purpose. In connecting with people from diverse backgrounds, they saw the infinite potential for learning and growth.

In their quest to follow their passions and embrace lifelong learning, Lily, Max, and Mia also uncovered the importance of stepping out of their comfort zones. The pursuit of one's passions often required taking risks, confronting fears, and challenging preconceived notions. It was about pushing boundaries and discovering the untapped potential within.

Stepping out of their comfort zones was evident when they ventured into the remote villages of Bhutan to experience a lifestyle radically different from their own. They embraced unfamiliar customs, engaged with local traditions, and even tried their hand at traditional crafts.

Lily's passion for environmental conservation led her to confront the reality of deforestation and the challenges faced by remote communities. She worked alongside locals, learned about their sustainable practices, and contributed to the preservation of the pristine Bhutanese forests.

Max, in his pursuit of technological innovation, found himself navigating complex projects and collaborating with individuals who spoke different languages and operated in unique cultural contexts. These experiences pushed him to adapt, think creatively, and communicate effectively in diverse environments.

Mia's passion for storytelling took her into uncharted territories, where she engaged with people who spoke languages she didn't understand and embraced traditions she had never encountered. She learned to navigate cultural differences, gaining a deeper appreciation for the power of communication and storytelling.

Their journey underscored that stepping out of one's comfort zone wasn't just a personal challenge; it was a gateway to personal growth and transformation. It was an opportunity to confront biases, dismantle stereotypes, and cultivate empathy for the diverse world that existed beyond their familiar borders.

As they followed their passions and continued to learn, the trio discovered that their individual pursuits were not isolated endeavors but interconnected facets of a shared dream. Their journey was a testament to the power of collaboration, where their unique passions converged to create a tapestry of experiences and insights that enriched their lives and those they encountered.

In the chapter on "Follow Your Passions," Lily, Max, and Mia were living proof that the pursuit of one's passions was not just a luxury but a fundamental part of the human experience. It was a journey of self-discovery, learning, and growth that transcended geographical boundaries and cultural divides.

Their experiences served as a reminder that passion was a force that could drive individuals to explore, connect, and transform the world around them. It was an invitation to embrace lifelong learning, step out of one's comfort zone, and embark on a path that resonated with the deepest desires of the heart.

The chapter on "Follow Your Passions" became a beacon of inspiration, urging readers to reflect on their own dreams and passions, to acknowledge the value of life-long learning, and to be willing to step beyond the familiar confines of comfort in the relentless pursuit of self-discovery and fulfillment.

Chapter 10: Preparing Your Mind for the Journey

In the grand tapestry of their global adventure, Lily, Max, and Mia had embarked on a journey that transcended geographical borders and explored the depths of human experience. Yet, in this immersive journey of self-discovery and learning, there emerged a pivotal chapter, "Preparing Your Mind for the Journey." This chapter encapsulated the profound understanding that, beyond the physical preparations and logistical details, the most important journey was the one undertaken within the corridors of the mind.

Their odyssey had been replete with rich experiences, cultural immersion, and encounters with diverse communities. They had ventured into the heart of sustainability in the Amazon Rainforest, engaged with tech innovation in Southeast Asia, explored the pages of history in ancient lands, and delved into the mysteries of happiness and fulfillment. Yet, the key to unlocking the treasures of their journey lay within their own minds.

As they ventured deeper into the world, it became evident that the state of their minds was paramount in shaping their experiences. The trio recognized that a mindset of openness, adaptability, and curiosity was the compass that guided them through the ever-changing landscapes of their journey.

The first lesson they learned about preparing the mind for the journey was the importance of embracing ambiguity and uncertainty. Traveling to unfamiliar places meant that they would often encounter situations that were entirely different from their daily lives. These experiences could be uncomfortable, challenging, and sometimes disorienting.

Instead of resisting the unknown, they embraced it as an opportunity for growth. They acknowledged that every encounter with ambiguity was a chance to learn, adapt, and expand their horizons. This shift in perspective allowed them to navigate even the most uncertain situations with grace and resilience.

Their journey was also a continual exercise in letting go. The nomadic life required them to detach from material possessions and familiar surroundings. It became an exercise in understanding that true freedom wasn't rooted in the accumulation of belongings but in the ability to detach and adapt to ever-changing circumstances.

Mia, who had always been a sentimental collector, found herself learning to let go of possessions that held sentimental value. It was a liberating experience that demonstrated the impermanence of material things and the importance of embracing the intangible moments and experiences that life had to offer.

Max, with his fascination for technology, recognized that the digital world he had been accustomed to was not a constant in their nomadic lifestyle. He had to let go of the need for constant connectivity and adapt to periods of limited access. In doing so, he found a deeper connection with the present moment and the people around him.

Lily, the passionate environmentalist, learned to let go of her expectations and attachments to specific outcomes in their efforts toward sustainability. She understood that nature followed its own rhythm, and their role was to observe, learn, and adapt rather than impose preconceived notions.

The concept of mindfulness was another cornerstone of their mental preparation. As they journeyed through diverse cultures, they embraced mindfulness as a tool for experiencing each moment fully. They learned to be present, to engage with their surroundings with curiosity, and to savor the richness of the present moment.

Mindfulness allowed them to appreciate the small details of their journey - the colors of a bustling market, the aroma of a foreign spice, the laughter of children in a remote village. It became a practice that enriched their experiences and deepened their connection with the world around them.

Their journey also revealed the power of adaptability. They encountered situations where their well-laid plans went awry, where language barriers presented challenges, or where they found themselves in unfamiliar environments. These were opportunities to cultivate adaptability, to think on their feet, and to find creative solutions.

Adaptability wasn't just about reacting to unexpected situations; it was also about embracing change as an inherent part of their journey. It was about being open to new ideas, perspectives, and experiences, even when they challenged their existing beliefs. It was a reminder that adaptability was a key to growth and resilience in an ever-changing world.

In their preparation, they recognized the significance of self-compassion. Travel, with its inherent challenges and uncertainties, could be both physically and emotionally taxing. Self-compassion became their inner anchor, a practice that allowed them to be kind and patient with themselves in the face of difficulties.

Mia, who had always been her harshest critic, learned to extend compassion to herself. She understood that the journey was a learning process, and it was okay to make mistakes and face setbacks. Self-compassion became a source of strength, allowing her to bounce back from challenges with resilience.

Max, with his drive for perfection, discovered the importance of self-forgiveness. He recognized that mistakes and imperfections were not shortcomings but opportunities for growth and learning. Self-compassion allowed him to maintain a sense of balance and well-being, even in the face of high standards and expectations.

Lily, as the environmental advocate, realized that self-compassion was a necessary tool for maintaining her passion and commitment. She understood that the work of sustainability was often met with resistance and setbacks. Self-compassion allowed her to stay true to her mission and continue her efforts with unwavering dedication.

The journey had been a profound exercise in empathy. As they ventured into diverse communities and interacted with people from different cultures, they found that empathy was a bridge that connected them to the hearts and minds of others. It allowed them to understand the perspectives of people whose lives and experiences were vastly different from their own.

Empathy was not just about understanding; it was also about actively listening, engaging in meaningful conversations, and creating connections that transcended language barriers. It was a practice that enriched their encounters and transformed strangers into friends.

One of the most powerful lessons they learned about preparing the mind

for the journey was the importance of gratitude. Their experiences had revealed the vast beauty of the world and the richness of human connections. Gratitude became a daily practice, a way to acknowledge the blessings that surrounded them and to find joy in the simplest moments.

They recognized that, in the grand scheme of things, their journey was a privilege, and they were grateful for the opportunities they had been given. Gratitude wasn't just a personal practice; it also became a way to give back to the communities they encountered. They engaged in acts of kindness, supported local initiatives, and contributed to the well-being of others.

In the chapter on "Preparing Your Mind for the Journey," Lily, Max, and Mia discovered that the most profound journey was the one undertaken within the mind. It was a journey of embracing ambiguity, letting go, practicing mindfulness, cultivating adaptability, and extending self-compassion.

It was a journey of empathy and gratitude, of understanding that the world was a diverse and wondrous place, and that every moment was an opportunity for growth and self-discovery. The chapter became a testament to the transformative power of a prepared mind, a mind that was open, resilient, and ready to embrace the endless adventures that awaited in the boundless horizons of their journey.

Conclusion: Finding the New American Dream

In the culmination of their extraordinary journey as digital nomads, Lily, Max, and Mia found themselves standing at the threshold of a realization that would forever redefine their concept of the American dream. Their quest had taken them far beyond the confines of traditional borders, exposing them to a world of experiences, cultures, and understanding that would fundamentally change their perspective on life, freedom, and fulfillment.

As they reflected on their journey, they discovered that the new American dream was not about acquiring wealth or possessions. It was about embracing the freedom to explore, learn, and live life to the fullest. It was a dream that celebrated the pursuit of happiness, the power of lifelong learning, and the value of human connections.

The trio had ventured far from their traditional classroom, beyond the confines of textbooks and the rigidity of standardized education. In doing so, they had unearthed a treasure trove of knowledge that wasn't limited to the pages of a curriculum but was interwoven into the fabric of the world itself. They realized that every corner of the globe was a classroom, and the act of learning was not restricted to a set schedule or location.

The new American dream was a testament to the importance of following one's passions. It was about recognizing that each individual possessed unique talents, interests, and dreams that were worth pursuing. Their journey revealed that these passions weren't mere luxuries but were, in fact, the compass that led them to a fulfilling and purposeful life.

They understood that life was too short to be spent on pursuits that didn't resonate with their hearts. The new American dream was about being brave enough to follow those dreams, no matter how unconventional or challenging they might seem. It was about embracing the journey as a lifelong learner, continually seeking knowledge, and pushing the boundaries of personal growth.

Their quest had opened their eyes to the significance of cultural understanding and tolerance. It became clear that the world was a rich tapestry of diversity, a mosaic of different languages, traditions, and ways of life. The new American dream celebrated this diversity, recognizing it as a source of strength and wisdom.

In a world where stereotypes and prejudices could create division, their journey had been a living example of the power of tolerance and understanding. It was about connecting with people from different cultures, breaking down barriers, and forming meaningful relationships. It was a reminder that, beneath the surface, there were more similarities than differences, and it was through these connections that true understanding could be achieved.

The new American dream also celebrated the importance of simplicity. In a consumer-driven society, where material possessions were often equated with success, their journey had revealed that true happiness couldn't be found in the accumulation of things. It was about embracing a minimalist approach to life, recognizing that the pursuit of materialism often led to a cycle of stress, debt, and the loss of freedom.

They understood that happiness was not a destination but a journey, a journey that could be found in the simplest experiences and the connections they formed with others. It was a reminder that the true value of life lay not in what one possessed but in the richness of experiences, the beauty of connections, and the depth of understanding.

Their chapter on "Nomadic Life on a Budget" had highlighted the importance of mindful spending and the value of budget travel. They had discovered that a fulfilling and budget-friendly nomadic life was not just a possibility but a reality that could be achieved by anyone with the right mindset and a passion for the world.

The new American dream was a reflection of their belief that a fulfilling life wasn't about the pursuit of endless possessions but about embracing simplicity, making conscious choices, and focusing on what truly mattered. It was about cooking meals in local markets, sharing stories with fellow travelers in hostels, and embracing the beauty of simple pleasures.

Their journey had been a testament to the power of adaptability and the readiness to embrace ambiguity. They had learned that the state of their minds was paramount in shaping their experiences. The new American dream was a reminder that, beyond the physical preparations and logistical details, the most important journey was the one undertaken within the corridors of the mind.

They had embraced ambiguity and uncertainty as opportunities for growth. They learned to let go of material possessions, recognizing that true freedom lay in the ability to detach from the need for constant acquisition. Their experiences with mindfulness had allowed them to be fully present in each moment, savoring the richness of the present.

They recognized that adaptability was not just about reacting to unexpected situations; it was also about embracing change as an inherent part of their journey. Stepping out of their comfort zones had been a gateway to personal growth and transformation. The new American dream celebrated the importance of self-compassion, recognizing that travel could be emotionally taxing and that self-kindness was an essential practice.

Empathy and gratitude became integral to their journey, connecting them to the hearts and minds of people they encountered and reminding them of the blessings that surrounded them. The new American dream celebrated the power of empathy and gratitude as practices that enriched their encounters and transformed strangers into friends.

As they stood on the threshold of their conclusion, Lily, Max, and Mia had discovered that the new American dream was not a fixed concept but a personal and evolving vision. It was a dream that celebrated the freedom to explore, the pursuit of passions, and the understanding and tolerance of diverse cultures. It was a dream rooted in the pursuit of happiness and the value of simplicity, a dream that embraced lifelong learning and prepared the mind for the journey.

Their journey had not only transformed their lives but had the potential to inspire others to embark on their own quest for the new American dream. The conclusion was not an endpoint but a gateway to new beginnings, an invitation to embrace the journey of self-discovery and fulfillment that awaited beyond the horizon. It was a reminder that the new American dream was not a distant dream but a living reality that could be found in the beauty of the world and the richness of human connections.

Author Bio:

Author Bio: Marcy Schaaf

Marcy Schaaf, hailing from Flint, Michigan, is a full-time digital nomad who has embarked on a remarkable journey, breathing life into her dreams and passion for writing, illustrating, and formatting children's books. With an indomitable spirit and a commitment to live life on her own terms, she's woven together a career that seamlessly blends her creative endeavors with the ever-evolving world of remote work.

Marcy's story is a testament to the power of embracing a life of exploration and self-discovery, unshackling herself from the constraints of a traditional 9-to-5 existence. As a digital nomad, she's not just a writer and illustrator; she's a modern-day explorer, charting new paths and navigating uncharted territories both in her travels and her creative work.

A prolific creator of children's books, Marcy's words and illustrations captivate young minds and hearts, transporting them to whimsical worlds of imagination and wonder. Her stories are more than just narratives; they're adventures that nurture a love for reading and learning in children.

In her quest to live life on her own terms, Marcy has found creative ways to sustain her nomadic lifestyle. She is not only a self-published author but has also utilized online platforms such as Upwork and Fiverr to connect with clients, offering her unique skills in formatting and design. Her ability to provide value to others through her work has not only supported her travels but has also allowed her to thrive while conducting her business in USD.

For Marcy, life as a digital nomad isn't just about wandering from place to place; it's about an intentional embrace of the world's diversity, a celebration of the freedom to explore, and an embodiment of the new American dream where one's work and passions can coexist harmoniously. Her journey demonstrates that, in this age of technology and connectivity, individuals can create their unique path to success while living life to the fullest.

Marcy's story is a source of inspiration for those seeking a life less ordinary. It's a reminder that dreams can be turned into reality with determination, creativity, and a willingness to embrace change. She's an author, an artist, and a symbol of living life by design, crafting her own narrative in the grand tapestry of the world.